Ed—

Thanks for lots of fine times on the water

Merry Christmas

Gordon

December 2003

Trout Stream Insects

Dick Pobst with his grandson Jake, looking at insects. (Photo by Chip Richards)

Trout Stream Insects
AN *ORVIS* STREAMSIDE GUIDE

DICK POBST

Lyons & Burford, Publishers

Printed in Hong Kong by C & C Offset Printing Co. Ltd.

10 9 8 7 6 5

Library of Congress Cataloging-in-Publication Data

Pobst, Dick.
    Trout stream insects : an Orvis streamside
guide / Dick Pobst.
        p.   cm.   Includes bibliographical
references.
    ISBN 1-55821-067-9 : $16.95
    1. Trout fishing—United States. 2. Trout—
Food. 3. Insects, Aquatic—United States. 4. Flies,
Artificial. 5. Stream fauna—United States. I. Title.
CIP   90-19798

CONTENTS

How to Use This Book   1

What Trout Eat   3

The Four Main Trout Stream Insects   7

Life Cycle of the Mayfly   10

The Eastern Hatches   22

The Western Hatches   42

Terrestrials   62

Life Cycle of the Midge   64

Life Cycle of the Caddisfly   66

Life Cycle of the Stonefly   76

Bibliography   80

Photographic Credits   81

Personal Hatch Records   82

Acknowledgments

I finished this project with a vastly increased respect for the following people, who were most generous in their assistance—these are some of the world's best practical entomologists and photographers. I owe them tremendous gratitude for their help: Carl Richards, Ted Fauceglia, Dave Hughes, Jim Schollmeyer, Fred Oswalt, Jim Gilford, Chip Richards, for photos; Ernie Schwiebert, Mike Lawson, for hatch tables; Gary LaFontaine, Bob McKeon, for illustrations; Rick Hafele, Fred Arbona, Rich Merritt, for entomology; Nancy Pobst, for helping to make it clear; Tom Rosenbauer, for the book's structure; Perk Perkins, for the book's concept.

—DICK POBST

HOW TO USE THIS BOOK

The first few chapters explain the nature of the major trout-stream insects. After you have read the introductory chapters, you will notice that the book is divided into Eastern and Western Hatches, Caddisflies, Stoneflies, and Midges.

If you are fishing east of the Mississippi, look to page 22, which explains the eastern seasons. Then look to the Eastern Hatch Chart. The hatch bars are coded by season. Each season has its color:

BLACK, for the early season of dark flies

YELLOW, for the yellow and tan flies that hatch in early summer

RED, for the big flies that hatch in midsummer

GREEN, for the tiny flies that hatch in the late summer and fall

All the pages detailing the hatches are color-coded to correspond. Each major hatch has a full page, with pictures of the dun, spinner, and nymph stage of each insect, along with hatching information and suggested fly patterns.

Each fly name is followed by **E**, if it is important in the eastern states, **M** for the midwestern states. The western hatch section shows **R** for the Rocky Mountain area, **S** for the western spring creeks, and **P** for the lower Pacific Coast areas.

In the western section, starting on page 42, there is a general Western Hatch Chart and a separate hatch chart for the spring creeks. All the spring creek flies are found on other rivers, but these particular flies are more important on spring creeks. Pages here are color-coded the same way as those for the eastern hatches.

A few of the most important caddis and stoneflies are listed in the hatch charts for the mayflies, but for further information you need to go to the chapters related to these flies.

In the back of the book there are pages on which you can record the hatch dates and major hatches in your area. No national listing or chart can cover all local variations, so you should observe and keep your own records—and go back to them over the years.

We believe that you will find using the visual clues shown in the color photographs here much easier and more productive than trying to use scientific techniques to identify flies. Get the size, color, wing markings, and number of tails, and within a short time you will be able to identify the important flies where you fish.

When you are ready to buy a fly, or tie one yourself, you may use one of the suggested patterns. Or you can approximate the size, color, and body conformation (mayfly spinner or dun, downwing caddis, and so forth) of the hatch in question. Hook sizes will be close to the most common size of a certain fly hatch—but feel free to go up or down a size if local experts so advise.

Being able to identify and match the insects on which trout feed can make fly fishing an extremely rewarding experience. We hope this book will make it easier for you to do so, and that it will increase your enjoyment of the sport.

WHAT TROUT EAT

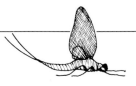

A few years ago, Carl Richards wrote an article called "The Practical Entomologist," which was one of the sources of inspiration for this book. He asked: "Why study entomology? Is it really that important? The answer to the latter is an emphatic yes, it is very important! The study of entomology will help us catch more and larger fish than would otherwise be possible."

A related observation was made by Ernie Schwiebert in his classic book, *Matching the Hatch.* "[The trout's] biggest advantage is selectivity, and we can counteract it only by knowing the insects that make up his diet. This is the reason for the study of stream entomology by the angler, and it is often the weak link in his skill. All of his other skills are aimed at getting the fly over a fish that is not yet aware of his presence. They are of little value if that carefully presented fly is not one that the trout wants. Stream tactics can be learned by experience, but stream entomology can be learned only by serious study."

The nature of both trout and trout-stream insects is that there are definite patterns of hatching; the trout discern those patterns and use them to feed selectively. So there are specific times and places when the fishing will be really exciting. Most trout feeding is done in connection with insect behavior.

Stream insects mature and hatch in batches. Once they have matured, they will hatch out at a particular time of year and a particular time of day. For example, the hendrickson flies hatch in the latter part of April in our area, and most often about the middle of the afternoon. The temperature of the season or the day may advance or retard this activity, but not much. Once the first few flies of this species have hatched, their classmates will continue hatching at about the same time of day, for two or three weeks, until they are all gone.

The fish respond to this pattern of behavior. Before a hatch of insects is visible on the surface, the nymphs will become active in the water and the fish will start to feed. Typically, they will begin a feeding spree that will go on until the last few of the insects have hatched, then start again when the insects return to the water to lay eggs. These sprees are the time when you are most likely to have exhilarating fishing. They are also the time the fish become most selective, and if you can't match the hatch you run the risk of getting skunked.

It is a happy circumstance that flies hatch, and fish feed, as Swisher and Richards told us, at the "pleasant time of the day." This is when the water and the air are neither too hot nor too cold. This means the activity takes place in the afternoon in the early spring and fall, the evening in the early summer, and at night when the summer gets too hot.

Temperature is probably the most important daily variable governing fly hatching and trout feeding. Peak hatching occurs when water temperatures are in the low 60s, and peak egg-laying occurs when the air temperature is in the high 60s or low 70s. By determining the times these temperatures will occur, you can get a pretty good idea about when the fish will feed. More detailed information on this subject can be found in Len Wright's book, *The Ways of Trout*. These peaks coincide pretty much with the "pleasant time of the day."

So, if you want to be a good fly fisherman, you have to understand what the trout eats, and why, and when. True scientific entomologies are useful to the very advanced angler. More practical are the angler's entomologies such as *Selective Trout,* by Doug Swisher and Carl Richards; *Hatches,* by Al Caucci and Bob Nastasi; *Caddisflies,* by Gary LaFontaine; the father of them all, *Matching the Hatch,* by Ernest Schwiebert, and several others. However, for many years we have been teaching a simpler approach to practical entomology. It minimizes the need for detailed entomology texts, microscopes, and Latin names. True, there is only so far you can go without knowing the Latin names, but you can start out without having to tackle them right away.

First, you should learn what the major flies in your area look like—before you go to the river. You should have a few of their imitations with you when you go. For example, I know that in my area on the opening day of trout season there are only three important fly hatches to reckon with: hendricksons, blue-winged olives, and little black caddis. I open this book to the dark-edged pages titled "Eastern Early Dark Flies," and can tell at a glance what the most important hatches will be, what they look like, and the sizes and patterns of artificial flies I need to have on the river. I can go to any good fly shop and find those flies, or reasonable substitutes, and be ready for the hatch. A knowledgeable shop manager will help me find the right ones. (There is no substitute for up to date local information.)

When I get to the river, if there are no rising fish or hatching flies, I will start fishing one of the nymphs until I start to notice some activity. As soon as I see flies hatching I will catch some and determine what they are. At this point, I do not need to know their names, only which of the flies in my early-season selection they most resemble.

This is the starting point. You can go as far as you like, but I am convinced of the validity of some early advice given me by Carl Richards: "Forget all the hundreds of flies. Concentrate on the dozen important hatches on your river, and get to know them well. Then you'll be light years ahead of most fishermen." By knowing the season, and by looking at the pictures of the flies for that season, my chances are well over 90 percent of being able to determine what hatches I might encounter, to identify the ones I actually do encounter, and to catch fish during a hatch. This is the interesting and exciting part of fly fishing and we hope this vest pocket guide will make it more fun and productive for you.

THE FOUR MAIN TROUT STREAM INSECTS

Mayflies *(Ephemeroptera)*

Upright wings are the most noticeable characteristic of this fly as it enters adulthood. Prominent tails sweeping back and upward and a curved body distinguish this fly from others. Most common sizes are bodies under ½-inch in length, although a few are up to 1 ½ inches, and a few down to ⅟₃₂-inch. These ephemeral flies are delicate in physical structure, dainty and graceful in flight, and perhaps one of the most beautiful creatures in existence. See page 10 for the complete life cycle.

Stoneflies *(Plecoptera)*

These robust flies feature resting adults with wings folded flat over the back. Two prominent short tails distinguish them from other flies, as do noticeable wing-case covers in the nymphs. Most have noticeable antennae, as well. Most have bodies ½-inch to 1-inch long, with wings a quarter to a third longer than the body. They are clumsy in flight, re-

7

sembling helicopters in their erratic, slow, and heavy flight patterns. See page 76 for the complete life cycle.

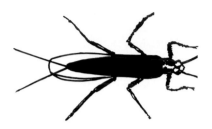

Caddisflies *(Trichoptera)*

These frenetic flies are very difficult to catch and identify. Adults have wings folded in the shape of pup tents when at rest, which is rare. Their most noticeable flight pattern is a frantic skittering over the surface of the water. Most have bodies of ¼-inch or less in length, but their wings are longer—50 percent to 166 percent longer—so they look much bigger in flight. See page 66 for the complete life cycle.

All these insects live most of their lives on the bottom of a stream or lake and sprout wings as adults. Only the caddis spin cases, like cocoons, by which they are often identified.

Midges *(Diptera;* family *Chironomidae)*

These tiny flies look just like mosquitoes, but have no beak
with which to bite. The term "midge" is often wrongly used
to mean any small fly. This is misleading and to be avoided.
Midges are often considered the least important of the
aquatic insects, yet they are abundant, and at times a sig-
nificant source of fishing opportunity. See page 64 for the
complete life cycle.

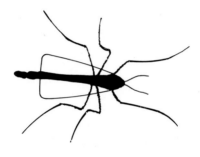

LIFE CYCLE OF THE MAYFLY

Mayfly eggs are laid on the surface of the water, most often in riffles, and frequently in the evening. This makes fishing the riffles in evening a productive method of fishing the mayfly.

The eggs hatch out into small insects called *nymphs*. These nymphs live most of their lives under water. The typical life span is one year.

At the end of the life cycle the nymphs hatch, usually by swimming up and attaching themselves to the surface film.

Then they shed their skins and sprout wings. These wings are typically gray, or *dun*-colored, which gives this stage of the insect's life its name: *dun*.

The wings are held upright over the back, so the duns look like little sailboats.

We suggest fishermen concentrate on identifying winged adults rather than nymphs. They are easier to identify and can quickly indicate which fly the fish are feeding on.

The dun, if it escapes the trout, flies away to the trees for a day or two to mature. When mature, the dun molts, its wings becoming cellophane-clear, and the body frequently darkens.

The flies then form into mating swarms over the river, swooping and swirling in the air, thus getting the name *spinner*. The spinners mate in midair.

The females lay their eggs on the surface of the river.

The flies then fall *spent,* or dead, to the surface, where they once again become food for the trout. Their wings and tails are spread flat on the surface, and the life cycle is complete.

Things to Notice about Winged Mayflies

From this point, we will refer to hook size, which indicates body size of the fly. Identification pages give the most common hook size and life-size silhouettes of artificial flies.

This mayfly dun has opaque dun-colored wings. Notice the two tails. The wings have no special markings; we call these wings "unmarked."

This spinner has clear wings, like all spinners. These

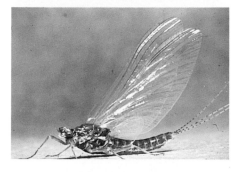

wings are also unmarked. This specimen has the small eyes

of the female. It has three tails.

This fly has blotched wings. Note the three tails.

This fly has barred wings and two tails.

Concentrate on identifying the adult flies. It is easier than identifying nymphs, and you can immediately match the hatch and, with a little luck, catch a fish.

Pronounce Latin names as you would Italian or Spanish. But you need not be too fussy; no one alive has ever heard ancient Latin as it was originally spoken.

Four Major Mayfly Nymph Types and Habitats

Knowing the nymph type helps you figure out what sort of water it lives in, and therefore, where the hatch will occur.

CLINGERS are strong and built flat so they can hold on to rocks in the fastest water. Rapids and tumbling water are

where they live. They need a lot of oxygen. Their heads are wide, their bodies flat, and their legs muscular in appearance. These include the *Stenonema* of the East, the *Epeorus* of East and West, and *Rhithrogena* and *Heptagenia* of the western rivers. They thrive where stoneflies live, which means they are abundant in mountain areas.

CRAWLERS are round-bodied, with round, narrow heads. They crawl around gravel and weeds. They are found in riffles where currents are moderate in speed. These may be the most important of the mayflies, including the hendricksons and sulphur duns of the East and pale morning and evening duns of the West, all of genus *Ephemerella*. They are common in spring creeks and gentle riffles all over the trout range. Other crawlers include the Tricos.

SWIMMERS are streamlined and narrow of body. They may be found in either fast, slow, or moderate water. They include the speedy *Isonychias*, the tiny olives, and the fascinating gray drakes, which lay their eggs in the fastest water and then hatch out of backwater eddies. *Callibaetis* are also among this group and are principally slow-water dwellers. Prominent gills help them swim.

BURROWERS have big tusks on their heads for digging. They dig burrows and tunnels in silt, sediment, and sand.

They include the giant mayflies, eastern green drakes, brown drakes, and other hatches. Mainly, they hatch out of slow water.

A Typical Twenty-Four-Hour Cycle

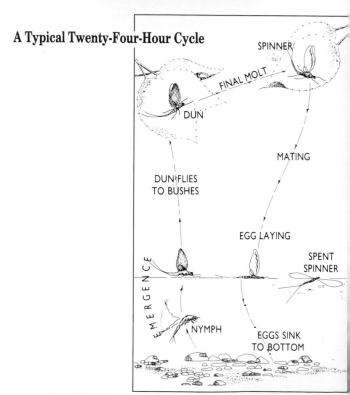

SPINNER

FINAL MOLT

DUN

MATING

DUN FLIES
TO BUSHES

EGG LAYING

SPENT
SPINNER

EMERGENCE

NYMPH

EGGS SINK
TO BOTTOM

HOOK SIZE CHART

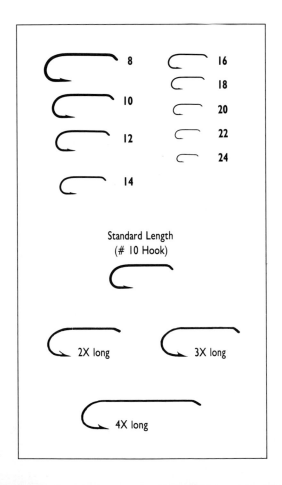

Standard Length
(# 10 Hook)

2X long

3X long

4X long

Artificial Flies

First row: Caddis Imitations

| Larva | Pupa | Adult | Diver |

Second row: Mayfly Imitations

| Nymph | Floating Nymph | Dun | Spinner |

Third row:

Tiny Mayflies   Midges

Thorax Olive   Trico Spinner   Pupa   Adult

First row:

Adams   Ausable Wulff   Thorax Light Cahill

Second row:

    Stoneflies   Sulphur Mayfly

Nymph   Adult

Third row:

Comparadun Mayfly   No-Hackle Dun Mayfly

Eastern Fly Hatches

PAGE	COMMON NAME	LATIN NAME	HOOK SIZE	MM	MAR	APR	MAY	JUN	JUL	AUG	SEP	OCT
24	QUILL GORDON	E. pleuralis	12	10								
26	BLUE-WING OLIVE	B. vagans	18	6								
29	LITTLE MAHOGANY	P. adoptiva	16	7								
27	LITTLE BLACK CADDIS	C. aterrima	16	7								
25	HENDRICKSON	E. subvaria	14	9								
29	BLACK QUILL	L. cupida	12	11								
28	MARCH BROWN	S. vicarium	12 2XL	15								
37	EASTERN GRAY DRAKE	S. quebecensis	12 2XL	13								
30	LARGE SULPHUR	E. invaria	16	7								
31	LITTLE SULPHUR	E. dorothea	18	6								
32	LIGHT CAHILL	S. canadense	14	9								
28	GRAY FOX	S. fuscum	12 2XL	13								
33	LITTLE YELLOW STONEFLY	A. chloroperla	12	10								
34	EASTERN GREEN DRAKE	E. guttulata	8 2XL	20								
29	LEADWING COACHMAN	I. bicolor	12 2XL	14								
35	BROWN DRAKE	E. simulans	10 2XL	13								
36	GIANT MAYFLY	H. limbata	8 2XL + 1/4"	25								
37	YELLOW DRAKE	E. varia	12 2XL	14								
37	GOLDEN DRAKE	P. distinctus	8 2XL	14								
38	SLATE-WING OLIVE	E. lata/attenuata	16	7								
40	WHITE-WING BLACK	T. strygiatus	24	3								
39	TINY BLUE-WING OLIVE	P. anoka	24	3								
41	WHITE MAYFLY	E. leukon	14	9								

Chart annotations: EARLY DARK FLIES · LIGHT FLIES · TINY FLIES · BIG FLIES

THE EASTERN HATCHES

The fly hatches east of the Mississippi are mainly different species of flies from those of the West. Additionally, climatic differences make for different hatching patterns. Therefore, we have divided the eastern and western flies.

While early- and late-season hatches occur during the day, most summer hatches and spinner falls occur in the evening, and to a lesser extent in the morning. The hatches can be divided into four seasonal groups:

THE EARLY, DARK-COLORED FLIES, that hatch mainly on spring afternoons, with spinner falls in the evening.

THE EARLY-SUMMER YELLOW (OR LIGHT) FLIES, that hatch late afternoons and evenings, with spinners falling up to dusk.

THE MIDSUMMER BIG FLIES, that hatch at or after dusk.

THE TINY FLIES, that hatch morning and evening during late summer, and afternoons in the fall.

The pages for these hatches are color-coded so you can quickly locate the likely hatches of the season.

QUILL GORDON E

Mayfly, *Epeorus pleuralis*

ADULT CHARACTERISTICS: Common hook size #12, two tails, unmarked wings, brown body.

HATCH: Late March, April. Duns hatch afternoon, spinners fall afternoon. Nymphs, clinger type, emerge under water from rapids and eddies. Spinners hover over rapids. Fast-water habitat requires good flotation for dry flies.

PATTERNS: Quill Gordon, Adams
Dun: Comparadun, unmarked gray wings, slanted back, brown body, split tails.

Spinner: Spent wing, wound hackle clipped top and bottom, split tails, brown body.

Nymph: Gold-Ribbed Hare's Ear, dark brown.

Emerger: Add full marabou wet-fly wing to nymph.

Hook size: #12

24

Eastern Early Dark Flies, Afternoon Hatches

HENDRICKSON E M
Mayfly, *Ephemerella subvaria*

ADULT CHARACTERISTICS: Hook size #14, three tails, unmarked wings, brown or tan body.

HATCH: Late April, May. This is the major hatch of the early season on most waters east of the Mississippi. Duns hatch afternoons, spinners fall evenings. Nymphs, crawler type, emerge from gravel riffles and emerge at surface, often floating as nymphs.

PATTERNS: Hendrickson
Dun: Thorax Hendrickson or No-Hackle Sidewinder, unmarked gray wings, light brown body, split tails.

Spinner: Spent-wing Swisher-Richards Hen Spinner, light hen wings, split tails, brown body.

Nymph: Common Hendrickson nymph, brown body, black wing pad.

Emerger: Same as nymph; should be fished dead-drift at surface.

Hook size: #14

BLUE-WINGED OLIVE
LITTLE BLUE QUILL E M
Mayfly, *Baetis vagans*

ADULT CHARACTERISTICS: Hook size #18, two tails, unmarked wings, tan to olive body.

HATCH: Duns hatch early April to late May, then sporadically through season. Duns emerge late morning to dusk, spinners fall afternoon or evening. Nymphs inhabit gentle riffles and runs containing vegetation.

PATTERNS: Thorax or No-Hackle Blue-Winged Olive, Adams
Dun: Gray wings, olive-brown body, split tails, minimum hackle.

Spinner: Light Hen-Wing Spinner, split tails, brown body.

Nymph: Olive-brown body, black wing pads.

Emerger: Add dark, short marabou feathers to nymph.

Hook size: #18

Eastern Early Dark Flies, Afternoon Hatches

LITTLE BLACK CADDIS
E M
Caddisfly, *Chimarra aterrima*

ADULT CHARACTERISTICS: Hook size #16, charcoal body, gray wings.

HATCH: Mid-April to mid-June. Late mornings and afternoons, emerges from gentle riffles and runs. Rides water as winged adult, easily fished.

PATTERNS: Downwing Little Black Caddis
Dun: Charcoal body, tent wings of gray quill, black hackle.

Spinner: Same as dun, but add bright green egg sac.

Pupa: Black Antron body, gray wings, black wet soft-hackle.

Hook size: #16

Eastern Early Dark Flies, Afternoon Hatches

MARCH BROWN E M
Mayfly, *Stenonema vicarium*

GRAY FOX E M
Mayfly, *Stenonema fuscum*

ADULT CHARACTERISTICS: Two-tailed, barred-winged flies, size #12 2XL. These two flies are almost identical, except that March Brown is dark brown (see dun) and Gray Fox is tan to gray (see spinner).

HATCH: May and June, hatching afternoon or evening, spinner fall evenings. Clinger types found in rapids. Flies migrate to slower water and hatch at surface. Both emergers and duns are effective.

PATTERNS: March Brown, Gray Fox **Dun:** Comparadun or Paradun, wings slanted back using barred flank feathers, two prominent split tails, tan or brown bodies.

Spinner: Spent wing, split tails, slightly bushy wing for flotation.

Nymph. Gold-Ribbed Hare's Ear.

Emerger: Add sprouting wings of flank feathers to the nymph.

Hook size: #12 2XL

Eastern Early Dark Flies, Secondary Hatches

BLACK QUILL
Mayfly, *Leptophlebia cupida*

Hook size #12; dark brown body, noticeable segments, unmarked wings, three tails; almost like hendrickson except larger, darker, and more rare. Late April, May.

LEADWING COACHMAN
Mayfly, *Isonychia bicolor, Isonychia sadleri*

Hook size #12 2XL; two tails, unmarked wings, dark body, four hind legs that are light-colored. Nymphs crawl from water and hatch on land. Heavy spinner falls evenings, mainly in the East. Late May, then sporadic.

RUSTY DUN
MAHOGANY DUN
Mayfly, *Paraleptophlebia adoptiva*

Hook size #16; dark mahogany body, unmarked wings, three tails; like hendrickson except smaller, darker, more rare. Late April, May.

OTHER EARLY DARK FLIES:
E. cornuta, E. needhami, P. mollis, P. debilis

Eastern Early Summer Light Flies, Late Afternoon and Evening Hatches

SULPHUR DUN E M
Mayfly, *Ephemerella invaria*

ADULT CHARACTERISTICS: Large sulphur, size #16, three tails, yellow body, unmarked wings.

HATCH: May and June. Nymphs emerge from gentle riffles and runs, often popping off so fast the fish have to settle for floating nymphs. Hatch late afternoon, spinner fall at dusk.

PATTERNS: Sulphur Dun, Pale Morning Dun, Pale Evening Dun
Dun: Split tails, yellow body, gray unmarked wings.

Spinner: Spent wing, dull yellow to brown body, wound-hackle wings clipped top and bottom.

Nymph: Size #16 Hendrickson-type nymph.

Emerger: Fish nymph in surface film.

Hook size: #16

Note: Ephemerella rotunda is almost identical. So is **Epeorus vitrea**, except it has two tails and no wing markings.

Eastern Early Summer Light Flies, Evening Hatches

LITTLE SULPHUR DUN
E M
Mayfly, *Ephemerella dorothea*

ADULT CHARACTERISTICS: Size #18, three tails, unmarked wings, yellow body.

HATCH: Hatch late May, June evenings, spinners at dusk. Nymphs often pop off so fast that fish will feed on floating nymph more readily than dun.

PATTERNS: Sulphur, Pale Evening Dun **Dun:** Thorax or No-Hackle, unmarked gray wings, split tails, yellow body.

Spinner: Rusty Spinner.

Nymph: Hendrickson type.

Emerger: Same as nymph; should be floated dead-drift at surface.

Hook size: #18

Eastern Early Summer Light Flies, Evening Hatches

LIGHT CAHILL E M
Mayfly, *Stenacron canadense*

ADULT CHARACTERISTICS: Size #14, yellow body, two tails, barred wings.

HATCH: Late May, June. Hatch and spinner fall evenings. Nymphs clinger type, inhabit rapids, migrate to slower water to emerge.

PATTERNS: Light Cahill
Dun: White wings, yellow body, white hackle, if any.

Spinner: Yellow body, split wings, sparse hackle wings.

Nymph: Tan nymph, light tan wing case.

Emerger: Floating nymph or flank-feather emerger.

Hook size: #14

Note: Related light flies are *Stenonema rubrum* and *S. heterotarsale*.

LITTLE YELLOW STONEFLY E M
Stonefly, Chloroperlidae family

ADULT CHARACTERISTICS: Size #12, yellow body, light wings down over back 1.3 times body length.

HATCH: Various species of small yellow stoneflies hatch continually throughout warm months and are important during lulls in other hatches.

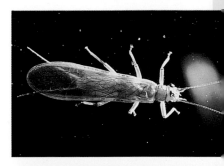

PATTERNS: Little Yellow Stone
Dun: None; stoneflies crawl out of water to hatch.

Spinner: Down-wing yellow stonefly. Egg-laying adult drops in moving water, rides the water, then flies away, so both dead-drift and moving down-wing flies will work.

Nymph: Yellow-bodied nymph, with two noticeable short tails.

Emerger: Same.

Hook size: #12

GREEN DRAKE E

Mayfly, *Ephemera guttulata*

ADULT CHARACTERISTICS: #8 2XL, three tails, cream body with green tint, splotched cream wings.

HATCH: Late May, mid-June. This hatch is the climax of the season for many eastern anglers. Hatches from sediment in slow pools or runs. Nymphs rise swiftly to surface, then struggle to emerge. Spinners fall in moving water. Hatch and spinner fall in evenings.

PATTERNS: Comparadun Green Drake Dun: Cream wings, tan deer-hair body provide visibility and flotation.

Spinner: Hen-Wing Spinner.

Nymph: Large hare's-ear nymph; fish by lifting from bottom.

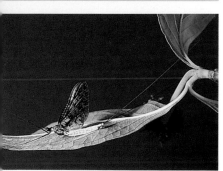

Emerger: Same as nymph. Douse unweighted nymph with floatant and fish dead-drift.

Hook size: #8 2XL

Eastern Midsummer Big Flies, Dusk or Evening Hatches

BROWN DRAKE E M W
Mayfly, *Ephemera simulans*

ADULT CHARACTERISTICS: #10 2XL, three tails, tan body, blotched brown wings.

HATCH: Mid-June to mid-July. Nymphs, burrower type, emerge from sand-gravel mixture in slow runs and gentle riffles. Hatch and egg-laying occur about dark.

PATTERNS: Brown Drake Paradun
Dun: White calf wing for visibility, tan deer-hair body, long split tails, parachute hackle.

Spinner: Wound-hackle wings, clipped; deer-hair body; long split tails.

Nymph: Hare's-ear nymph.

Emerger: Nymph fished in surface film.

Hook size: #10 2XL

GIANT MAYFLY M

Mayfly, *Hexagenia limbata*

Note: A similar large fly is *H. (Litobrancha) recurvata*.

ADULT CHARACTERISTICS: #8 2XL with ¼-inch body extension. Two tails, tan body, 1¼ inches to 1½ inches long, unmarked wings. Burrower.

HATCH: Late June, early July, from black silt in slow water. Night fishing during this hatch is a major experience in angling. Most hatching and egg-laying is after dark. Spinners fly far upstream to lay eggs in moving water.

PATTERNS: Giant Mayfly
Dun: Paradun, white hairwing, parachute hackle, extended body on long-shank #8 hook, split tails.

Spinner: Clipped wound-hackle wings, deer-hair body, split tails, or substitute white calf tail for wings and tails.

Nymph: Hare's ear.

Emerger: Nymph. Douse fly in flotant and fish in film.

Hook size: Long-shank #8 2XL with ¼-inch body extension

Eastern Midsummer Big Flies, Secondary Hatches

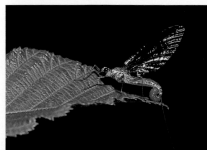

YELLOW DRAKE
Mayfly, *Ephemera varia*

Hook size #12 2XL; related to and similar to brown and green drakes, this yellow fly has three tails and wing blotches. Hatches at dusk, mid-June, July. Yellow paradrake, rusty spinner.

GRAY DRAKE
Mayfly, *Siphlonurus quebecensis, S. alternatus, S. rapidus*

Hook size #12 2XL; this could be the most underrated hatch of the East. From mid-May to mid-July these spinners congregate in huge clouds, but only at or after dark, and only over rapids or strong riffles. The fish know about them, but most anglers do not. The fly has a slim body with a ring around the eye. Two tails. Slim-bodied rusty spinner.

GOLDEN DRAKE
Mayfly, *Potamanthus distinctus*

Hook size #8 2XL; this light yellow fly has three tails and barred wings. Hatches at dusk in slow water. Egg sac apparent on female spinner. Paradrake, rusty spinner.

LITTLE DARK OLIVE E M
Mayfly, *Ephemerella lata,*
Ephemerella attenuata

ADULT CHARACTERISTICS: Size #16, unmarked wings, brown body, three tails. Crawler.

HATCH: Mid-July to mid-August. Emerges morning from riffles; spinners fall evening in riffles.

PATTERNS: Blue-Winged Olive, Adams
Dun: Thorax tie, brown body, gray wings, split tails.

Spinner: Hen-Wing Spinner.

Nymph: Hendrickson.

Emerger: Float nymph dead-drift at surface.

Hook size: #16

Eastern Late-Season Tiny Flies, Daytime Hatches

LITTLE BLUE-WINGED OLIVE E M

TINY BLUE QUILL

Mayfly, *Pseudocloeon anoka*

ADULT CHARACTERISTICS: Size #24, two tails, unmarked wings, olive body.

HATCH: Mid-July, September. Swimmer type, inhabits gentle runs with vegetation. Hatch morning, spinners fall in evening.

PATTERNS: No-Hackle Blue-Winged Olive

Dun: Olive body, gray wings sidewinder style, split tails.

Spinner: Spent wings, olive body, split tails.

Nymph: Little Olive Nymph.

Emerger: Nymph fished in film.

Hook size: #24

TINY WHITE-WINGED BLACK, TRICO E M

Mayfly, *Tricorythodes stygiatus*

ADULT CHARACTERISTICS: Size #24 tied short; black body, white wings, three tails.

HATCH: If you want to be a really good fisherman, learn to master this hatch. The flies are tiny, they hatch in bright weather, and the fish are hard to fool. Hatch in slow runs with vegetation and silt from late July into October. Duns hatch early in morning, with spinners mating immediately after.

PATTERNS: Trico

Dun: No-Hackle, white wing, black body, split tails.

Spinner: Spent wing, but some prefer an upright tuft for visibility.

Nymph: Small and black.

Emerger: Nymph fished at surface.

Hook size: #24

40

Eastern Late-Season Secondary Hatches

WHITE MAYFLY
Mayfly, *Ephoron leukon*

When we tire of fishing tiny flies, a new evening hatch occurs with #14 white flies hatching and then laying eggs, all in the same evening. From mid-August to mid-September they provide very nice fishing at and after dusk. Three tails. White thorax dun, white spinner.

Western Fly Hatches

PAGE	COMMON NAME	LATIN NAME	HOOK SIZE	MM	MAR	APR	MAY	JUN	JUL	AUG	SEP	OCT
46	WESTERN MARCH- BROWN	R. morrisoni	14	9	P							
47	LITTLE OLIVE	B. tricaudatus	18	6	P							
48	SLATE MAROON DRAKE	E. nitidus	14	9								
48	GREEN (GRAY) SEDGE	R. pellisa, coloradensis, bifila	14									
48	SLATE GRAY DUN	E. Longimanus	14	9								
49	PALE MORNING DUN	E. inermis	18	6								
50	PALE MORNING DJN	E. infrequens	16	7								
51	SALMON FLY	P. californica	10 6XL	40		P						
52	WESTERN GREEN DRAKE	E. grandis	10 2XL	15								
53	BROWN DRAKE	E. simulans	10 2XL	13								
54	SMALL WESTERN DRAKE	E. flavilinea	14	9								
54	SPOTTED SEDGE	H. occidentalis	14			P						
61	SLATE CREAM DUN	E. albertae	16	7								
61	WESTERN RED QUILL	H. elegantula	16	7								
56	SPECKLE WING QUILL	C. coloradensis, nigritus	16	7		P						
55	WESTERN GRAY DRAKE	S. occidentalis	12 2XL	14								
57	WHITE-WING BLACK	T. minutus	24	3								
58	TINY BLUE QUILL	B. parvus	22	4								
60	MAHOGANY DUN	P. bicornuta	18	6								
59	TINY BLUE-WING OLIVE	P. edmundsi	22	4								

EARLY DARK FLIES — LIGHT FLIES — BIG FLIES — TINY FLIES

THE WESTERN HATCHES

The tremendous differences in climate, altitude, and latitude in the western United States and Canada create great differences in hatching times.

As in the East, there is still a pattern of: dark flies, light flies, big flies, and tiny flies. However, many of the dark flies hatch before and during runoff and so are not often fishable in the mountains. Also, the light flies start hatching before the big flies, and continue afterward.

THE DARK FLIES, then, are important at lower altitudes or for those who fish before snow-melt. These include the march browns and early olives. The hatches of importance on the Pacific Coast are marked **P.**

THE LIGHT FLIES start hatching during runoff, then continue for most of the summer. These include the pale morning duns, (*Ephemerellas*). The flies of major importance in the mountains are marked **R.**

THE BIG FLIES hatch in latter May and June on the Pacific Coast, late June and July in the mountains. These include the western green drake, the salmon fly, and the golden stone.

TINY FLIES. Because average temperatures are cooler over more of the West than they are in the East, a large portion of hatching activity occurs during the day, with evening (and morning) activity occurring mostly during the warmest parts of the season.

Spring Creek Hatches

PAGE	COMMON NAME	LATIN NAME	HOOK SIZE	MM	MAR	APR	MAY	JUN	JUL	AUG	SEP	OCT
47	LITTLE OLIVE	*B. tricaudatis*	18	6								
49	PALE MORNING DUN	*E. inermis*	18	6								
50	PALE MORNING DUN	*E. infrequens*	16	7								
52	WESTERN GREEN DRAKE	*E. grandis*	10 2XL	15								
53	BROWN DRAKE	*E. simulans*	10 2XL	13								
56	SPECKLE-WING QUILL	*C. coloradensis, nigritus*	16	7								
57	WHITE-WING BLACK	*T. minutus*	24	3								
58	TINY BLUE QUILL	*B. parvus*	22	4								
60	MAHOGANY DUN	*P. bicornuta*	18	6								
59	TINY BLUE-WING OLIVE	*P. edmundsi*	22	4								

EARLY DARK FLIES

LIGHT FLIES

P

BIG FLIES

TINY FLIES

The Western Spring Creeks

Hatch activity on the western spring creeks needs to be separated from other rivers.

Spring creeks are spring-fed. They tend to be moderate to slow in current speed, rich in lime content, and fairly uniform in temperature. They are warmer in the spring and fall, and cooler in summer, than are other rivers.

Because of constant temperatures and water chemistry, spring creeks produce huge numbers of the same insect species over a longer period than is possible in other rivers.

For these reasons they have fewer of the clingers and stoneflies, which require faster water, and more of the smaller crawlers and swimmers. Important spring-creek hatches are marked **S.**

These streams produce prodigious quantities of flies, so the fish are well fed. They are also highly selective because the waters are typically clear and free from tumbling. Fly imitations have to be more natural, and they do not require as much flotation.

These spring creeks are the biggest challenge to the angler, requiring lots of skill, but promising ample rewards. Large fish can be taken on properly fished floating flies during daylight hours, and there is constant hatch and feeding activity.

WESTERN MARCH BROWN R P

Mayfly, *Rhithrogena morrisoni*, *Rhithrogena hageni*

ADULT CHARACTERISTICS: Hook size #14, two tails, mottled wings, brown body.

HATCH: March, early April. Like most western early dark flies, much of the hatch occurs before and during snow-melt. Nymphs, clinger type, hatch from rapids or migrate to slower eddies. Spinners return to rapids. This fly is related and similar to eastern march brown, with two tails, but the wings are blotched instead of barred.

PATTERNS: March Brown

Dun: Parachute March Brown, brown body, split tails, mottled wings.

Spinner: Spent wing, split tails. Wings of wound cree hackle or deer hair will provide mottling.

Nymph: Dark-colored hare's ear, or Wiggle Nymph

Emerger: Hafele's March Brown Flymph.

Hook size: #14

Western Early Dark Flies, Afternoon Hatches

LITTLE OLIVE R P S

IRON BLUE QUILL
Mayfly, *Baetis tricaudatis*

ADULT CHARACTERISTICS: Hook size #18, two tails, unmarked wings, olive body.

HATCH: April-May, and again in September-October. Nymphs, swimmer type, live in moderate currents with weeds, especially in spring creeks: emerge midday or afternoon. Spinners fall afternoon or evening.

PATTERNS: Blue-Winged Olive
Dun: No-Hackle Sidewinder, split tails, olive body.

Spinner: Swisher-Richards Hen-Wing Spinner, split tails.

Nymph: Simplest dark olive body.

Emerger: Floating nymph, olive body, short split tails.

Hook size: #18

47

SLATE MAROON DRAKE R
Mayfly, *Epeorus nitidus*

Related to eastern quill gordon, with two tails and unmarked wings. Hatches morning or midday from rapids or eddies. #14 Adams Wulff.

SLATE GRAY DUN R
Mayfly, *Epeorus longimanus*

#14 gray-bodied relative of above with two tails and unmarked wings. Fast-water habitat. Gray Wulff.

Western Light Flies

PALE MORNING DUN
R P S
Mayfly, *Ephemerella inermis*

This pale morning dun begins to hatch during the big-fly season. Different authorities vary on hatch times of various species; however, the pale morning dun group of hatches are among the most important hatches in the West. They are of the same family and genus, but species and sizes vary.

The most common size of the earliest to hatch is #18. All the pale morning duns are dull yellow to light olive in color. They are very similar to the eastern sulphur duns. All have three tails and unmarked wings.

These are among the most important of the spring-creek flies. No-Hackle, Parachute, or Thorax Pale Morning Duns and hen spinners for the adults, and nymphs or floating nymphs for the emergers. Hook size #18.

PALE MORNING DUN
P R S
Mayfly, *Ephemerella infrequens*

ADULT CHARACTERISTICS: Size #16 or #17, three tails, unmarked wings, dull yellow body.

HATCH: Nymphs inhabit moderate riffles, emerge in daytime, spinners fall morning. Very important on spring creeks.

PATTERNS: Pale Morning Dun
Dun: No-Hackle Pale Morning Dun.

Spinner: Hen-Wing Rusty Spinner.

Nymph: Hare's ear.

Emerger: Floating nymph.

Hook size: #16 or #17

Western Big Flies

SALMON FLY P R
Stonefly, *Pteronarcys californica*

Both the nymph and adult of the stone-fly have the same robust body, the adult form adding wings. Common body sizes are from 1 inch to 1½ inches. #10 6XL. Hatches June and July in the mountains, April and May on the coast.

The fish see this fly as a nymph crawling around bottoms in the fast water, as it crawls out of the water in the evening or at night, then as the winged adult as it returns to lay eggs in fast water or as it is blown into the water on windy days.

The nymph should have a segmented black body, blackish brown wing-case segments, prominent short dark tails and antennae. The body should be soft to touch, as is the natural. Dave Whitlock's Stonefly, Box Canyon Stone, Randall Kaufmann or Jim Teeny nymph patterns.

The adult should be the same, with wings about 25 percent longer than the body. Improved Sofa Pillow pattern, with salmon-colored belly.

GIANT GOLDEN STONE
Stonefly, *Calineuria californica*

This fly is similar in size and habits to the salmon fly, but is golden in color and starts hatching a few weeks later.

WESTERN GREEN DRAKE
P R S

Mayfly, *Ephemerella grandis*,
Ephemerella doddsi

ADULT CHARACTERISTICS: Size #10 2XL, three tails, unmarked wings, green body; may be described as portly.

HATCH: Hatches occur during the day on faster spring creeks and moving freestone rivers. May be the most important single hatch of the West for fish and fishermen. Wings can emerge under water. Spinners apparently fall at night because they seem rare to anglers. The nymph is a crawler.

PATTERNS: Green Drake
Dun: Mike Lawson's Green Paradrake.

Spinner: Fat-bodied spinner.

Nymph: Fat dark hare's ear.

Emerger: Flymph.

Hook size: #10 2XL

52

Western Big Flies

BROWN DRAKE R S
Mayfly, *Ephemera simulans*

ADULT CHARACTERISTICS: Size #10 2XL, three tails, blotched wings, tan body (brown in the spinner).

HATCH: Burrowing nymphs inhabit slower silty water with sand and gravel mixture. Duns hatch and spinners fall at dusk. The body is much slimmer than that of the green drake, which can overlap in hatch times.

PATTERNS: Brown Drake
Dun: Brown Paradrake or Comparadrake. Deer-hair body, prominent split tails.

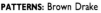

Spinner: Wound clipped-hackle wings, long widely split tails.

Nymph: Wiggle-tail tan nymph.

Emerger: Floating nymph, doused so that the entire body floats in the surface film.

Hook size: #10 2XL

SLATE-WING OLIVE R S

SMALL WESTERN DRAKE

Mayfly, *Ephemerella flavilinea*

ADULT CHARACTERISTICS: Size #14 green-bodied fly, with three tails and unmarked wings.

HATCH: Hatches during the day from late June through August; resembles and follows green drakes, but smaller. Spinners fall morning, sometimes evening.

PATTERNS: Blue-Wing Olive
Dun: Thorax Slate-Wing Olive.

Spinner: Hen-Wing Rusty Spinner.

Nymph: Hare's ear.

Emerger: Floating nymph.

Hook Size: #14

Western Big Flies

WESTERN GRAY DRAKE
P R
Mayfly, *Siphlonurus occidentalis*

ADULT CHARACTERISTICS: Size #12 2XL, two tails, gray body with brown markings, unmarked wings.

HATCH: This fly hatches August to October. It lives in slow waters and lays eggs in moving water. The nymphs, swim to slow water before hatching. Spinners morning and evening. Duns may hatch at night.

PATTERNS: Gray Drake
Dun: Gray Paradrake.

Spinner: Wound hackle trimmed top and bottom, gray body, split tails.

Nymph: Hare's ear, fished along edges.

Emerger: Same as nymph.

Hook size: #12 2XL

SPECKLED QUILL R S

Mayfly, *Callibaetis coloradensis, Callibaetis nigritus*

ADULT CHARACTERISTICS: Size #16; two-tailed brown-bodied fly has unique wing markings as its prime characteristic. Wings can look like window panes or can be blotched.

HATCH: August 10 to October 10. This is a slow-water fly that hatches from lakes or slow streams, especially spring creeks. Duns hatch midday, spinners fall morning and evening.

PATTERNS: Speckled Spinner
Dun: Speckle-Wing Paradun.

Spinner: Wound grizzly hackle, tan body.

Nymph: Unribbed hare's ear.

Emerger: Same as nymph, fished swiftly rising.

Hook size: #16

Western Tiny Flies

WHITE-WING BLACK, TRICO P R S
Mayfly, *Tricorythodes minutus*

ADULT CHARACTERISTICS: Size #24, three tails, unmarked wings, black body.

HATCH: Mid-July to October; duns hatch early morning, spinners fall immediately after. Nymphs inhabit slow to moderate currents, including spring creeks. Duns change to spinners within an hour.

PATTERNS: Trico
Dun: No-Hackle or parachute dun.

Spinner: Wound hackle or poly-wing spinner.

Nymph: Simple black body.

Emerger: Flymph or floating nymph.

Hook size: #24

LITTLE BLUE QUILL P R S
Mayfly, *Baetis parvus*

ADULT CHARACTERISTICS: Hook size #22, two tails, unmarked wings, olive body.

HATCH: Mid-August through October, emerging early afternoon. Spinners fall at dusk. The fly inhabits moderate currents and spring creeks.

PATTERNS: Blue-Wing Olive
Dun: Thorax or No-Hackle.

Spinner: Hen-Wing Rusty Spinner.

Nymph: Simple little olive body.

Emerger: Floating nymph.

Hook size: #22

Western Tiny Flies

TINY BLUE-WING OLIVE
P R S
Mayfly, *Pseudocloeon edmundsi*

ADULT CHARACTERISTICS: Size #22, two tails, unmarked wings, olive body.

HATCH: July 15 to October 15; emergence in afternoon, spinners fall evening. Moderate currents and spring creeks.

PATTERNS: Blue-Wing Olive
Dun: No-Hackle or Thorax olive fly, split wings.

Spinner: Hen-Wing Rusty Spinner.

Nymph: Simple olive body.

Emerger: Floating nymph.

Hook size: #22

MAHOGANY DUN P R S
Mayfly, *Paraleptophlebia bicornuta*

ADULT CHARACTERISTICS: Size #18, three tails, unmarked wings, brown body.

HATCH: Hatches late August to October from gentle riffles in rivers and spring creeks. Emerges morning, spinners fall evening.

PATTERNS: Mahogany Dun
Dun: Thorax or No-Hackle Mahogany Dun.

Spinner: Hen-Wing Mahogany Spinner

Nymph: Small Hendrickson pattern.

Emerger: Floating nymph.

Hook size: #18

Western Secondary Hatches

SLATE CREAM DUN R P
Mayfly, *Epeorus albertae*

This light-colored mayfly inhabits faster waters at lower altitudes. Hatch occurs from July 5 to August 15 and emergence is at dusk; spinners fall morning and evening. Hook size #16. Two tails. Tan comparadun, rusty spinner.

WESTERN RED QUILL R P
Mayfly, *Heptagenia elegantula*

This darker fly also occurs at lower altitudes, emerging mornings with spinner falls in the evenings. Hatch occurs from August 5 through September 25. Hook size #16. Two tails. Brown comparadun, rusty spinner.

TERRESTRIALS

Grasshoppers become active and fly around the fields on warm summer days. They get blown into streams by the wind and the trout key in on them as a source of food, thereby creating an event as exciting as a fly hatch.

ANTS AND BEETLES get blown off streamside bushes and create a steady source of food for the fish. Watch for trout feeding regularly underneath overhanging bushes.

INCHWORMS also get blown off bushes. Each of the terrestrial insects tends to be active at a particular time, and you will want to watch for that activity. Shake a bush to see what's up.

LIFE CYCLE OF THE MIDGE

Midges are so tiny that they get little attention from the angler, but trout can zero in on them and take them to the exclusion of much larger flies.

Midges hatch in the water and live the best part of their lives as larvae on the bottom of the stream.

Like caddis, they turn to pupae before emerging as adults. These pupae float for long distances, hanging on the under-

side of the surface film, before hatching. The pupa is the form most fed on. When midges are active, fish a pupa of the proper size and body color in the surface film.

Midges may be the least important of the aquatic insects, but there are times when they are *very* important.

LIFE CYCLE OF THE CADDISFLY

Caddisflies spend the larval stage in cocoons, called cases; in nets like spiderwebs, which they spin; or crawling among rocks on the bottom of the stream.

Larvae are typically two hook sizes larger than the later stages. Some of these larvae drift or are available to the trout for plucking off the bottom.

When ready to emerge, the larvae change into pupae that use their legs and wings and bodies to swim to the surface.

They are easy pickings for the trout at this point. The pupae may drift a long distance attached to the surface film. This is the caddisfly's most vulnerable stage.

Adults hatch from the pupae and in many cases fly away instantly. Splashy rises by the trout indicate the fish are afraid the fly will escape.

Egg-laying females may drop their eggs on the surface, fly

to the surface to deposit eggs, swim to the bottom to lay eggs, or crawl into the water. Their behavior is complicated, and both dry flies and winged wet flies are used to imitate the egg layers.

Flying caddis are most easily noticed by their frantic skittering over the surface of the water.

The trout see the body of the caddis and will key in on its color. Wing color, pattern, and shape are important in identifying the caddis, but of little significance to the trout. As with most aquatic insects, the silhouette and size are most important. Wings should be from 150 percent to 200 percent of the body length. With the exception of some early- and late-season flies, bodies of brown-yellow, olive, and bright green will cover most hatches.

See the Bibliography for further information about caddisflies.

Some Basic Caddis Patterns

Accurate identification of caddisflies is a very, very tricky and difficult business. There are hundreds and perhaps thousands of species. They are very hard to catch. Few of the country's top entomologists can identify an adult fly, even when they see it. No one at present has anything resembling a complete set of photos of the important adult flies, to help identify the natural insects.

Therefore a different approach is required. It is most practical simply to carry some of the common patterns and attempt to approximate the flies you see on the water.

For that reason, we have prepared the following lists of common patterns for the East and the West, with Gary LaFontaine's help. For each hatch you need larvae, pupae, adults, and divers. Descriptions are for body color/wing color. For example, tan/gray means tan body, gray wing.

Eastern Caddisfly Selection

LARVA	Green/Brown	#12, #14
LARVA	Cream/Brown	#12, #14
PUPA	Green/Tan	#14, #16, #18
PUPA	Olive/Tan	#16, #18
PUPA	Tan/Tan	#14, #16, #18

DIVER	Green/Tan	#16, #18
DIVER	Olive/Tan	#16, #18
DIVER	Tan/Tan	#16, #18
ADULT	Green/Tan	#16, #18
ADULT	Olive/Tan	#16, #18
ADULT	Tan/Tan	#12, #14 #16, #18
ADULT	Black/Gray	#16

Western Caddisfly Selection

LARVA	Green/Brown	#12, #14
LARVA	Cream/Brown	#12, #14
PUPA	Green/Tan	#14, #16, #18
PUPA	Olive/Tan	#14, #16, #18
PUPA	Tan/Tan	#14, #16, #18
DIVER	Green/Tan	#14, #16, #18
DIVER	Olive/Tan	#14, #16, #18
DIVER	Tan/Tan	#14, #16, #18
ADULT	Green/Tan	#14, #16, #18
ADULT	Olive/Tan	#14, #16, #18
ADULT	Tan/Tan	#14, #16, #18, #20
ADULT	Yellow/Black	#18

Special patterns are needed for *Dicosmoecus* in fall.

The Caddis Super Hatches

Even though it is difficult to sort out the caddisflies, the available literature does indicate that most authorities have selected some of the same hatches as being most important in the trout fishing areas of North America. They are listed

below, along with sketches from *Caddisflies,* which will help
you determine which flies, or at least which families of flies,
are available.

Type of cases or nets that are really numerous in your
streams will help you predict which flies will hatch in numbers. You can use the sketches of adult flies at least to make
a stab at using the identification clues:

Length of antenna
Shape of wing
Wing markings

While hatch periods for caddisflies are long, there are
some that can be characterized as spring, summer, or fall
flies. Use this list in conjuction with the available books to
learn more about caddisflies.

Eastern Caddisflies

Chimarra aterrima

little black sedge, #16

(family Philopotamidae, finger-net builder)

April, May. Pupa, emergence, and egg-laying occurs afternoon at surface.

Black body, gray wing.

Brachycentrus numerosus

American grannom, #16

(family Brachycentridae, chimney-tube casemaker, rapeller,
second in importance nationwide)

May. Green body, tan wings. Emerges afternoon, egg-laying evening at surface.

Glossosoma nigrior

little tan shorthorn sedge, #18

(family Glossosomatidae, dome casemaker)

Greenish brown body, tan wing common on May-June hatch.

Rhyacophila fuscula, Rhyacophila manistee

green rock worm, green sedge, #14, #16

(family Rhyacophilidae, free living, builds no case. May be third in importance nationwide)

May, June. Olive body, mottled wing. Inhabits and emerges from fast water; dives to lay eggs, then drifts back to surface.

Psilotreta labida E

dark blue sedge, #14

(family Odontoceridae, sand-tube casemaker)

Late May, June. Green body, gray wing. Pupa emerges quickly; eggs are laid at the surface, the female flopping as she lays them.

Hydropsyche morosa E, *Hydropsyche slossonae* M

spotted sedge, #18

(family Hydropsychidae, net spinner, rapeller, first in importance nationwide)

Tan-body mottled-wing flies active June, July. Pupae drift at surface to emerge, females dive to bottom to lay eggs, then drift back to surface.

Pycnopsyche guttifer E, *Pycnopsyche lepida* M

great brown autumn sedge, #12

(family Limnephilidae, stick-tube casemaker)

Large caddis with ginger body and mottled wing occurs late summer and fall. Emerges morning and evening; egg-layers swim to bottom or lay eggs along banks.

Western Caddisflies

Hydropsyche occidentalis, Hydropsyche cockerelli

spotted sedge, #14

(family Hydropsychidae, net spinner, rapeller, first in importance nationwide)

H. occidentalis mid-May, mid-July; *H. cockerelli* late season. Brownish yellow body, mottled wing. Pupae drift at surface, egg-layers are active at surface, dive, then drift back to surface.

Rhyacophila pellisa, Rhyacophila coloradensis,
Rhyacophila bifida

green sedge, gray sedge, #14

(family Rhyacophilidae, free living, may be third in importance nationwide)

Late June, July. Olive-green body, mottled wing. Inhabits and emerges from fast water, dives to lay eggs, then drifts back to surface.

Cheumatopsyche campyla, Cheumatopsyche pettiti

little sister sedge, #16

(family Hydropsychidae, net spinner, rapeller, of major importance in large fertile waters, including tailwaters)

June, August (during salmon-fly hatch). Green body, mottled tan wing.

Brachycentrus occidentalis, Brachycentrus americanus

American grannom, #14

(family Brachycentridae, tube casemaker, rapeller, second in importance nationwide)

B. occidentalis April, May (before runoff); *B. americanus* July, August.

Green body, tan wing. Emerges and lays eggs midstream, either floating or diving.

Lepidostoma pluviale

little brown sedge, #16

(family Lepidostomatidae, tube casemaker)

June to August. Tan body, tan wing. Much emerging and egg-laying occurs along water edges.

Oecetis disjuncta, Oecetis avara

longhorn sedge, #14

(family Leptoceridae, tube casemaker)

O. disjuncta June; *O. avara* mid-June, mid-August. Brown-yellow body and wing. Prefers slow water.

Amiocentrus aspilus

little western weedy water sedge, #18

(family Brachycentridae, tube casemaker)
Late June. Greenish brown body, brown wing. Prefers weedy spring creeks.

Mystacides alafimbriata

black dancer, #18

(family Leptoceridae, tube casemaker)

Late June, July. Yellow body, black wings. Pupae crawl out, egg-layers dive to bottom around dusk.

Discosmoecus jucundus, Dicosmoecus gilvipes, Dicosmoecus atripes

giant orange sedge, #8 2XL

(family Limnephilidae, tube casemaker)

September, October. Reddish orange body, mottled wings. Emerges afternoon, lays eggs evening. Drifting larvae important in summer.

LIFE CYCLE OF THE STONEFLY

The stonefly is the simplest to fish of all the flies. It is available to the fish in only two stages: the nymph and the egg-laying adult.

The nymphs usually inhabit fast water and rapids, where the clinger mayflies abound. They are easily identified because they have two short prominent tails.

The nymphs crawl from the water to hatch on land, and the trout follow them in their migration.

Adults look exactly like the nymphs with the addition of wings that fold flat over their backs when at rest. In flight they look like little helicopters, clumsy and lumbering. They fly to the river to lay eggs and are available to the trout as food at that stage.

Stoneflies

genus *Allocapnia* E, genus *Capnia* W

tiny winter black, #16

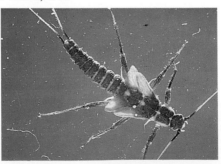

Among the most important foods of steelhead, the nymphs emerge during midwinter.

genus *Taeniopteryx* E W, genus *Brachyptera* W

---

early black, early brown, #10
Late-winter emergences of major importance to steelhead.

Pteronarcys californica W, *Pteronarcys dorsata* E

---

giant black, #10 6XL
The salmon-fly hatch of the West is a superhatch by any standard.

Phasganophora capitata E, *Paragentina media* M, *Acroneuria lycorias* M, *Acroneuria pacifica* W, *Acroneuria californica* W, *Claasenia sabulosa* W

Giant Golden, #10 4XL
(family Perlidae)
Giant golden stones accompany the salmon-fly hatch in time and importance.

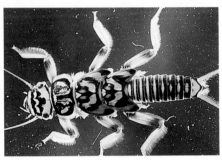

genus *Isogenus* W, genus *Isoperla* E

medium brown, medium yellow, #8 2XL
(family Perlodidae)

genus *Alloperla,* genus *Chloroperla*

little yellow, little green, #10
(family Chloroperlidae)
The smaller stoneflies fill gaps in the hatches throughout
the summer.

BIBLIOGRAPHY

Useful Books for Further Study

Caucci, Al, and Bob Nastasi. *Hatches II.*

———. *Instant Mayfly Identification Guide.*

———. *Comparahatch.*

Hafele, Rick, and Dave Hughes. *The Complete Book of Western Hatches.*

Hughes, Dave. *Western Streamside Guide.*

LaFontaine, Gary. *Caddisflies.*

Merritt, R. W., and K. W. Cummins. *An Introduction to the Aquatic Insects of North America.*

Schwiebert, Ernest. *The Flyfisher's Calendar.*

———. *Matching the Hatch.*

———. *Nymphs.*

Solomon, Larry, and Eric Leiser. *The Caddis and the Angler.*

Swisher, Doug, and Carl Richards. *Selective Trout.*

Swisher, Doug, Carl Richards, and Fred Arbona. *Stoneflies.*

Wright, Leonard. *The Ways of Trout.*

Videos

Borger, Gary. *Tying Trout Flies.*

Dennis, Jack. *Tying Western Flies.*

LaFontaine, Gary. *Tying and Imitating Caddis Flies.*

Richards, Carl, Dick Pobst, and Steve Spengler. *Super Hatches.*

Swisher, Doug. *Tying the Hatch Simulator Flies.*

PHOTOGRAPHIC CREDITS

A book like this would have been impossible without the superb photographs from all the contributors listed below, and without the helpful line drawings.

Robert McKeon drew all the line drawings and silhouettes in this book except for those on pages 72, 73, and 75.

Carl Richards: 10(T), 11(B), 14(T), 16, 17(T), 18, 25(T), 25(M,B), 26(T,B), 27(T,B), 28(M,B), 29(M), 30(T, M,B), 31(T,M,B), 32(T,M,B), 33(T,B), 34(T,B), 35(T,M,B), 36(T,B), 37(M), 38(M,B), 40(T,M,B), 48(T,B), 49(T), 50(T,M,B), 51(T,M,B), 52(T,B), 53(T,M,B), 54(T,M), 55(T), 56(T,M,B), 57(B), 59, 60, 61(T,B), 64(T), 66(B), 67(T,B), 68(B), 76, 77(T,B), 78(T,B), 79

Fred Oswalt: 10(B), 11(T)

Dick Surette: 20, 21

Ted Fauceglia: 12(T), 13(T), 15(B), 24(T,M), 26(M), 28(T), 29(M,B), 34(M), 37(T,B), 38(T), 39(T,B), 41, 47(M), 54(B), 62(T,B), 63, 65, 66(T), 68(T)

Jim Schollmeyer: 12(B), 13(B), 47(B), 49(M,B), 55(M), 57(T, B), 58(T, B)

Jim Gilford: 24(B), 29(T)

Dave Hughes: 17(B), 36(M), 46(T,M,B), 47(T), 52(M), 55(B), 64(B)

Harvey Eckert drew the drawings on pages 71, 72, 73, 75. They are reproduced from *Caddisflies* by Gary LaFontaine.

T=top M=middle B=bottom

Personal Hatch Records

DATE	TIME OF DAY	PLACE	HATCH	WEATHER/ WATER

Personal Hatch Records

DATE	TIME OF DAY	PLACE	HATCH	WEATHER/ WATER

Personal Hatch Records

DATE	TIME OF DAY	PLACE	HATCH	WEATHER/ WATER

Personal Hatch Records

DATE	TIME OF DAY	PLACE	HATCH	WEATHER/ WATER

Personal Hatch Records

DATE	TIME OF DAY	PLACE	HATCH	WEATHER/WATER

Personal Hatch Records

DATE	TIME OF DAY	PLACE	HATCH	WEATHER/ WATER

Personal Hatch Records

DATE	TIME OF DAY	PLACE	HATCH	WEATHER/ WATER

Personal Hatch Records

DATE	TIME OF DAY	PLACE	HATCH	WEATHER/WATER

Personal Hatch Records

DATE	TIME OF DAY	PLACE	HATCH	WEATHER/ WATER